GRATITUDE HEALS

A Journal for Inspiration and Guidance

LINDA ROSZAK BURTON

Published with the support of Publishing Partner, www.publishingpartner.com

Cover by Dara Stoltzfus

ISBN-13: 978-0-578-48152-4

DEDICATION

This journal is dedicated to my husband Mark, a.k.a. Bruno, our children Lauren and John, and our loving family and friends, for whom I am most grateful. Most especially, to my sister Debbie, who was and still is my inspiration and one of the greatest blessings in my life.

I hope this *Gratitude Heals*® journal will serve as a comprehensive resource to create and sustain a practice of expressing gratitude and make a lasting difference in your life and in your personal gratitude journey. Wishing you good health and happiness.

With gratitude,

TABLE OF CONTENTS

"Acknowledging the good that you already have in your life
is the foundation for all abundance."
—*Eckhart Tolle*

If you, someone in your family, or a friend is a victim of rape, abuse, or incest, seek help from a health professional. An additional resource may be the toll-free, 24-hour National Sexual Assault Hotline, 1-800-656-HOPE (1-800-656-4673), or https://www.rainn.org If you are in immediate danger, call 911.

If you are overwhelmed by stress and difficult challenges, seek help from a health professional. If you are in crisis, an additional resource may be the toll-free, 24-hour National Suicide Prevention Lifeline at 1-800-273-TALK (1-800-273-8255). For deaf and hard of hearing, call 1-800-799-4889. https://suicidepreventionlifeline.org/

If you or someone in your family is facing mental and/or substance use disorders, seek help from a health professional. An additional resource may be the toll-free, 24-hour Substance Abuse and Mental Health Services Administration helpline at 1-800-662-HELP (1-800-662-4357). https://www.samhsa.gov/find-help/national-helpline

INTRODUCTION

There could be several reasons why you picked up this journal. It could be the cover spoke to you and created a sense of calm or a promise of hope at the beginning of a new day. It's quite possible the word **Heals** captured your attention, considering the seemingly constant exposure to negativity, fear, and skepticism in daily life. Perhaps you instinctively responded to the word **Gratitude,** sensing the need to count your blessings, show gratefulness to others, and connect with something meaningful in life. Whatever the reason, ***thank you***, and give yourself credit for being attuned to something positive, proactive, and restorative.

From an early age, we're taught to say "thank you" as part of proper etiquette. For many of us in the United States, the Thanksgiving holiday symbolizes gratitude and one day to reflect on all we have to be thankful for in our lives. Unfortunately, the day after Thanksgiving, that state of gratitude can quickly disappear when someone pulls in front of you, taking the last parking place for Black Friday shopping, or someone reaches over your shoulder and grabs the last (insert the latest gizmo) off the shelf after you waited in line for eight hours before the store opened. Such an experience can leave you feeling angry for hours, casting a shadow over what started out as a positive and exciting excursion. That's a prime example of how fleeting positive emotions are and how negative experiences stay in your consciousness for a long time.

In this journal, I introduce the terms "gratitude practice" and "the practice of gratitude." Much like the practice of mindfulness, where we pay deliberate attention to the present, the practice of gratitude honors a deliberate thought process, a ritual, routine, or approach. Various techniques and resources are shared in this journal to support your practice of gratitude.

My own practice of expressing gratitude became more focused and sustainable as I began bringing the latest research and evidence-based practices into my executive coaching business. As I established many of the same concepts with my clients, and now as part of this journal, I began to personally experience the benefits discovered through existing research and studies. So much so, that to my great surprise, I was able to recontextualize my grief over losing my sister Debbie to breast cancer at the early age of 41, and soon after, the passing of my mother and father. I always thought of myself as being grateful, and yet when I looked back over my personal journaling, I recognized my thinking (writing) was still very dark, all about the grief, loss, and despair. The epiphany I experienced through my practice further strengthened my personal healing process. Your healing process, from whatever brings you pain, may be different from mine or may have a similar discovery.

My "Aha!" moment is what inspired me to write this journal. I hope to share what I've learned in my research, minimize the scientific lingo, and offer you the flexibility to practice gratitude in the ways that feel most natural. To that end, I've created content by translating the research and best practices on gratitude, positive psychology, and neuroscience into something you can use in your daily life.

You'll notice the img4™ (I am grateful for) icon throughout this journal. The concept of img4 started at our kitchen table years ago. The research was so compelling that a greater awareness and emphasis on gratitude quickly became a family ritual: A small whiteboard placed in the middle of the table quickly filled with messages of gratitude, ranging from thankful expressions for a great cup of coffee to mindful reflections of our health and happiness. Since that time, our whiteboard experience has strengthened and broadened our own personal practice of expressing gratitude, and we give img4 whiteboards to family and friends. Today, we openly share our experiences and practice techniques in our personal and professional lives.

I hope this journal will inspire and guide you in your personal adaptation and learning experiences of expressing "practicing" gratitude. With a sustainable practice, gratitude can heal a deep wound, help turn the corner in recovery, lessen the impact of depression or post-traumatic stress, and build strength in the face of a terminal or chronic illness. And in turn, you can begin to gain greater emotional, spiritual, mental, and physical resilience, find hope again, and rediscover meaningful relationships. Practicing gratitude gives us hope, strength, energy, wisdom, and the serenity to meet life's many challenges of grief, anxiety, depression, loneliness, and fear.

Your feedback on this journal is welcomed and appreciated. Please take a few minutes to forward your thoughts, insights, likes or dislikes, and any additional information you would like to see included. Email me at lburton@drwcoaching.com

"Gratitude bestows reverence, allowing us to encounter everyday epiphanies, those transcendent moments of awe that change forever how we experience life and the world."
—John Milton

BREATHE IN LOVE - EXHALE GRATITUDE

WHAT IS GRATITUDE?

"Gratitude is a vaccine, an antitoxin, and an antiseptic.
A vaccine against the invasion of a disgruntled attitude.
An antitoxin against the poison of fault-finding and grumbling.
A soothing antiseptic in the spirit of thanksgiving."
—John Henry Jowett

Gratitude has been defined as a strength of the heart, a pathway to greater health and well-being, and the parent of all virtues. To live gratefully, to have a broader orientation toward gratitude, has been linked to a stronger bond with our local communities, more satisfying relationships, and greater resilience in the face of adversity and trauma.

To give you a framework for a stronger foundation in your practice, let's start with a review of some of the key research findings and science in the fields of gratitude, positive psychology, and the neuroscience involved.

Gratitude—So, what is gratitude exactly? With all the associated definitions, the answer is—it depends. Historically, many religious, spiritual, and philosophical references on gratitude existed long before modern social scientists began their research. Today, however, we are fortunate to have a greater understanding of the science of gratitude. In this journal, we'll move beyond the theoretical framework of the research and validated measurements into a more meaningful and purposeful use to support the outcomes you hope to achieve and to guide you through the development of your own practice of gratitude.

Based on a review of the research, gratitude is categorized in several ways. First, being in a state of gratitude. The emotion we feel when someone has helped us (the technical term is a gratitude intervention). Second, "trait gratitude," which is the frequency and ease with which we experience gratitude. In his book, *Gratitude Works!* (2013), Robert A. Emmons, PhD, describes gratitude as an affirmation of goodness and a recognition of goodness outside ourselves. So, gratitude is much more than feeling thankful. It is a profound appreciation of what is good in our lives, which in turn creates greater awareness and positivity. And, it must genuinely represent someone or something of value and meaning in our lives.

Dr. Emmons describes "dispositional gratitude" as including:

- Span—the number of things an individual is grateful for;
- Frequency—how often an individual is grateful;
- Intensity—the depth of feeling over the benefit received;
- Density—the number of people an individual is grateful for, for a particular benefit.

Positive Psychology—Positive psychology is defined as the scientific study of how our strengths enable individuals and communities to thrive. It calls on a greater awareness of strengths, relationships, and positive emotions to truly flourish in life. In the positive psychology arena, gratitude is defined as a strength, enhancing our happiness and well-being. And yet, positive psychology is *not* the absence of pain and suffering or denying the negative. Later in this journal, you'll be asked to recall a time of sadness, grief, or unhappiness and consider the people and resources that helped you through a difficult period in your life. This type of "remembering the bad" technique is particularly helpful in recovery and building resilience for difficult life events to come.

The Neuroscience of Gratitude—With the growing body of research on gratitude, positive psychology, and the latest studies in neuroscience, we have a greater understanding of how to achieve and sustain the associated health and well-being benefits. Specifically, with advances in functional magnetic resonance imaging, or fMRI, modern neuroscience can observe what brain activity "looks like" when gratitude is being experienced. Once thought of as a simple emotion, fMRI has clearly shown that gratitude activates multiple regions of our brain, including those for moral reasoning, fairness, economic decision-making, and psychological well-being.

"What flows through your mind sculpts your brain."
—*Rick Hanson,* Buddha's Brain

More good news—neuroplasticity is the brain's ability to form new neural connections throughout life. Through your gratitude practice, you'll activate these "gratitude" circuits and strengthen the neural pathways in the brain. Just think about how easy it is to only notice the negative—those neural pathways are well traveled because we're hardwired to see the negative. Our primitive brain still functions as it did when cavemen and cavewomen roamed the earth. The opposite is true with creating more attention to what is going right and expressing what we have to be grateful for, thus strengthening existing pathways or creating new ones.

Gratitude also blocks toxic emotions. It's impossible to be angry and grateful at the same time. Our brains simply don't work that way. When we shift our brain's focus to gratitude, our change in thinking leads us to engage in more positive emotions and achieve better, healthier outcomes in our personal and professional lives.

Perhaps you've heard the statement "neurons that fire together wire together." The stronger our gratitude circuitry becomes, the more hopeful we become, and the better equipped we are to cope, heal, and reenergize ourselves.

Throughout this journal and universally, the terms "gift/benefit" and "giver/receiver" are used in the practice of expressing gratitude. For us to feel grateful, the gift we receive must feel genuine and fulfill something we truly value. In turn, this allows us to recognize the sacrifice or effort made by the giver for us, on our behalf.

Self-Gratitude—In this journal, you'll also discover the concept of self-gratitude. Some will argue that self-gratitude is wrong and too self-focused, and that gratitude is only meant to be externally focused. We'll take the liberty of including expressions of self-gratitude, genuinely and humbly and as an essential element of self-compassion. If we believe in the notion that we must love ourselves to love others, then why not the same with gratitude? In the end, it is this author's experience that self-gratitude takes us back to a gift or giver.

A few final thoughts about what gratitude is and isn't. The opposite of gratitude is entitlement. If someone believes they arrived where they are in life without the help and resources of others, it is unlikely that they will ever discover gratitude. Also, keep in mind that gratitude is not indebtedness. If you feel beholden to someone who has done something for you, you'll probably never fully experience the benefits of gratitude. Instead you'll have this sense of "I owe you" hanging over your head and weighing heavily on the relationship. And finally, gratitude is never about what you have that someone else does not. It's not a competitive sport!

> *"What separates privilege from entitlement is gratitude."*
> —*Brené Brown*

On a final note, the power of gratitude is **transformational**, and the research continues to inform us on how to achieve the associated benefits. You've probably heard of the 21-day gratitude challenge or listened to Oprah share how gratitude has changed her life. There is growing interest and resources, including this journal, to help kick-start and sustain your gratitude journey. DON'T give up. Make a commitment to develop your practice. If you stop writing journal entries, don't judge yourself; simply go back, review, and begin again!

BREATHE IN LOVE - EXHALE GRATITUDE

WHY GRATITUDE MATTERS

"There's a gratitude circuit in your brain, badly in need of a workout.
Strengthening that circuit brings the power to elevate your physical
and mental health, boost happiness, improve sleep,
and help you feel more connected to other people."
—*Alex Korb,* The Upward Spiral

Sounds like a magic pill, doesn't it? Which is why this journal is designed to capture the relevant and growing body of research being done in gratitude, positive psychology, and neuroscience overall. With this continued research and its broader appeal to health and well-being, the findings have become more mainstream and applicable in our homes, schools, communities, and work environments.

According to research, by having a sustained gratitude practice, our overall health and well-being improve over time. Gratitude:

- Fosters higher levels of positive emotions;
- Supports greater life satisfaction, vitality, and optimism;
- Enables more hours of sleep;
- Fosters better exercise habits and better care of our health;
- Strengthens the immune system, lowers blood pressure, reduces symptoms of illness, increases pain thresholds;
- Improves heart health by reducing levels of several inflammatory biomarkers.

Several studies indicate favorable changes to our biochemistry, including the production of the hormone dehydroepiandrosterone (DHEA), the "anti-aging" hormone. Additionally, several neurochemicals—dopamine, serotonin, and oxytocin—are released in our bloodstream when we write, reflect on, or express gratitude. Although the effects of these neurochemicals remain in our system for only short periods of time, they do act as an antidepressant, help motivate us, and also inhibit the stress hormone cortisol.

And, whether we're expressing gratitude for what's good in life or showing gratitude to someone who has helped us, our brain (stem) releases dopamine, which makes us feel good! Dopamine triggers positive emotions, so we feel optimistic, and it drives prosocial behaviors (behavior intended to help others). What's more, dopamine has been linked to the helpful, intrinsic motivation in goal accomplishment, whether academic, personal, or professional.

Serotonin is another neurochemical boost we receive from the brain when we reflect on the positives in life, whether it's something positive about work or about what someone has done for us. It enhances our mood (think antidepressant), our willpower, and our motivation. And yes, serotonin has also been called the happy molecule and the leadership chemical. Who could complain about that?

In addition, a release of the neurochemical oxytocin comes from receiving or giving a "gift" in gratitude that creates stronger social bonds, and it also builds trust and a feeling of safety. It's considered the glue that binds meaningful, healthy, and important relationships.

"The negative screams at you but the positive only whispers."
—*Barbara Fredrickson*

Something else wonderful happens to both the receiver and the giver. The receiver experiences a "pay it forward" response and becomes motivated to give someone else a similar sense of elevation (an uplifting feeling). Additionally, our brains are wired with mirror neurons. That means when someone expresses gratitude to us for something we've done, we "mirror" the same elevating emotions they are feeling. A double dose, so to speak, as both the giver and receiver experience a positive impact.

There is also growing research in the role gratitude plays in our having more resilience when dealing with today's difficult and often challenging life experiences. Psychologists define resilience as a commitment to find purpose in whatever's happening, to believe in your ability to create a positive outcome, and to be better prepared for the inevitable setbacks that occur. Easier said than done, and yet practicing gratitude is proving to be essential in creating greater resilience and leading to such positive outcomes as:

- Greater mental and emotional well-being;
- Greater resilience to trauma;
- Lower rates of post-traumatic stress disorder (PTSD) and an increased sense of purpose;
- Lower levels of depression and stress.

During a time of crisis, we often have the most to gain in having a grateful perspective on life. Being grateful is a choice. When things are bad, when we're suffering, when devastating events occur, a grateful attitude and perspective are hard to achieve. And yet, with practice, gratitude gives you the power to energize, to heal, to bring hope, and to help you cope with hard times. At some point in your awareness and in your gratitude practice, it's helpful to remind yourself of the people and resources—your own and those of others—that helped you through a difficult time.

"As human beings, part of our job is to be able to recognize what causes pain, to work toward healing, and to learn how to live in the world with empathy, forgiveness, and gratitude."
—*Diana Butler Bass*

Even with the impressive research on the health and well-being benefits of gratitude, there appears to be a deficiency in how we think about and express gratitude. A national survey commissioned by the John Templeton Foundation (a philanthropic catalyst for discoveries relating to the most perplexing questions facing humankind) identified this deficiency as a *gratitude gap*. The survey found that while 90 percent of respondents consider themselves grateful, only 52 percent of the women and 44 percent of the men surveyed **express** gratitude on a regular basis.

What if we had a gratitude map to begin closing the gap? A pathway to a practice technique that includes recognizing, appreciating, and acknowledging, the gift, giver, and all derived benefits. A way to ensure our individual practices are heartfelt, genuine, and sustainable. To help close this gap, go to the **Gratitude MAPS** activity in the Resource section of this journal (on page 163) to develop a framework for your practice and attain greater healing, health, and well-being.

BREATHE IN LOVE - EXHALE GRATITUDE

TIPS ON HOW TO MAKE THE MOST OF THIS JOURNAL

Current research indicates journaling is one of the most highly recommended ways to practice gratitude. And yet, if it feels like a chore or another item on your to-do list, there's less opportunity to achieve long-term benefits. Try writing in this journal two, maybe three times a week, or pick one day a week to capture your feelings of gratitude for three to five people, events, or things you found most meaningful. Use the img4 (I am grateful for) acronym to spur your journal entries. Don't limit yourself to just writing. Include drawing, sketching, and painting as alternate ways to express gratitude.

Greater health and well-being benefits are derived when you acknowledge the true value of something or someone in your life and how you have benefited by experiences or an individual's actions. When writing in this journal, remember to be as specific as possible in your descriptions.

Here are a few practice techniques to help you tap into the health and well-being benefits:

- Use this journal;
- Not into writing journal entries? Try visual journaling. Tap into the right side of your brain and draw, sketch, and paint to capture your expressions of gratitude (stick people work too!);

- Write down three good things that went well in your day or week and explain why they happened;
- Mindfully make a list of all the people in your life that you're grateful for and create journal entries describing why;
- Use the Gratitude Letter activity in the Resource section (on page 166), and write a letter of gratitude to someone, deliver it to them, and *read* it to them;
- Practice using the Gratitude MAPS activity in the Resource section (on page 163) to sustain your practice and the benefits;
- Use the Three Easy Steps activity in the Resource section (on page 167) to kickstart your practice;
- Use the prompts and quotes throughout this journal to inspire and guide how you think about and express gratitude.

From time to time you may find yourself staring at these blank pages and feeling like you have nothing new to write. Consider the following:

- Refresh a past gratitude entry. It's okay to repeat the same messages from time to time. Add more specifics to refresh your message by asking why something happened or why it's important;
- Create a self-gratitude entry. For example, name one of your top strengths and explain why you're grateful for that strength;
- Consider an absence of positivity—reflect on what your life would be like if you hadn't met your spouse, best friend, or colleague;
- Remember the bad as you practice journaling. Recall a challenging time or loss of a loved one and reflect on where you are today. Create gratitude entries about who and what resources made that journey possible.

Additionally, you'll find coaching prompts throughout this journal to further support your gratitude practice.

Finally, refer to the Resource section of this journal for self-administered assessments, books, websites, and videos to support your practice.

BREATHE IN LOVE - EXHALE GRATITUDE

I AM GRATEFUL FOR...

img4

_____

_____

_____

_____

_____

_____

_____

_____

_____

_____

_____

_____

_____

_____

_____

_____

_____

_____

Create a routine for Gratitude MAPS—Schedule a deliberate practice technique to reinforce your commitment to action. Schedule time on your calendar (every Friday morning, for example) or find a gratitude buddy and set up a regular practice routine.

DATE   /   /

I AM GRATEFUL FOR...

img4

_____

_____
_____
_____
_____
_____
_____
_____
_____
_____
_____
_____
_____
_____
_____
_____
_____
_____
_____

"I cannot pretend I am without fear.
But my predominant feeling is one of gratitude."
—*Oliver Sacks,* Gratitude

I AM GRATEFUL FOR...

img4

DATE   /   /

I AM GRATEFUL FOR...

I AM GRATEFUL FOR...

I AM GRATEFUL FOR...

img4

I AM GRATEFUL FOR...

img4

Absence of positivity—Think what your life would be like if you hadn't met your best friend, your significant other, or your neighbor. Journal about the gifts you have received from these special relationships.

I AM GRATEFUL FOR...

img4

"The struggle ends when gratitude begins."
—Neale Donald Walsch

DATE   /   /

I AM GRATEFUL FOR...

img4

DATE   /   /

I AM GRATEFUL FOR...

img4

I AM GRATEFUL FOR...

img4

I AM GRATEFUL FOR...

img4

I AM GRATEFUL FOR...
img4

Remember the bad—Remembering the bad is a good thing.
What were the resources, both internal and external, that helped
you through a difficult time? Reflect on them as you journal.
How have you become more resilient?

I AM GRATEFUL FOR...

img4

"*When you are grateful, fear disappears and abundance appears.*"
—*Anthony Robbins*

I AM GRATEFUL FOR...

img4

I AM GRATEFUL FOR...

img4

DATE / /

I AM GRATEFUL FOR...

img4

I AM GRATEFUL FOR...

img4

I AM GRATEFUL FOR...

img4

Who inspires you and why? Be as specific as possible in journaling how this
inspiration or this person has made a difference in your life.

I AM GRATEFUL FOR...

img4

> "Living a life of gratitude is healing energy."
> —Unknown

I AM GRATEFUL FOR...

img4

I AM GRATEFUL FOR...

img4

I AM GRATEFUL FOR...

I AM GRATEFUL FOR...

img4

I AM GRATEFUL FOR...

img4

Do you have a favorite family ritual? Write, specifically, about the benefits
you've received because of this ritual.

I AM GRATEFUL FOR...

DATE   /   /

_____

_____

_____

_____

_____

_____

_____

_____

_____

_____

_____

_____

_____

_____

_____

_____

_____

_____

"Gratitude is one of the most medicinal emotions we can feel.
It elevates our moods and fills us with joy."
—Sara Avant Stover

I AM GRATEFUL FOR...

img4

I AM GRATEFUL FOR...

img4

I AM GRATEFUL FOR...

img4

I AM GRATEFUL FOR...

img4

I AM GRATEFUL FOR...
img4

Reflect on one of the happiest days in your life. Consider what made that possible. Express your gratitude for the experience.

DATE   /   /

I AM GRATEFUL FOR...

img4

"Let gratitude be the pillow upon which you kneel
to say your nightly prayer."
—Maya Angelou

I AM GRATEFUL FOR...

I AM GRATEFUL FOR...

img4

I AM GRATEFUL FOR...

img4

I AM GRATEFUL FOR...

I AM GRATEFUL FOR...

img4

> What was one positive emotion you felt today? Write about it and express why you're grateful for the experience.

I AM GRATEFUL FOR...

img4

_____

_____

_____

_____

_____

_____

_____

_____

_____

_____

_____

_____

_____

_____

_____

_____

_____

_____

_____

_____

_____

"Persist in gratitude and you will slowly become one with the Sun of Love, and Love will shine through you its all-healing joy."

—*Rumi*

I AM GRATEFUL FOR...

I AM GRATEFUL FOR...
img4

I AM GRATEFUL FOR...

img4

DATE   /   /

I AM GRATEFUL FOR...

img4

I AM GRATEFUL FOR...
img4

What is it about your physical health that you are grateful for? Start with the simplest aspect. Write a description and express your gratitude.

I AM GRATEFUL FOR...

img4

_____

_____

_____

_____

_____

_____

_____

_____

_____

_____

_____

_____

_____

_____

_____

_____

_____

_____

_____

"When we focus on the loving gratitude we have for our pet, our heart opens and establishes coherence for our energetic and material body."
—Dr. Dennis Thomas

I AM GRATEFUL FOR...
img4

I AM GRATEFUL FOR...

img4

I AM GRATEFUL FOR...

I AM GRATEFUL FOR...

DATE   /   /

I AM GRATEFUL FOR...

img4

_____

_____

_____

_____

_____

_____

_____

_____

_____

_____

_____

_____

_____

_____

_____

_____

_____

_____

_____

_____

_____

_____

What is it about your mental health that you are grateful for? Start with the simplest aspect. Write a description and express your gratitude.

I AM GRATEFUL FOR...

img4

_____

_____

_____

_____

_____

_____

_____

_____

_____

_____

_____

_____

_____

_____

_____

_____

_____

_____

"At times our own light goes out and is rekindled by a spark from another person. Each of us has cause to think with deep gratitude of those who have lighted the flame within us."
—*Albert Schweitzer*

I AM GRATEFUL FOR...
img4

I AM GRATEFUL FOR...
img4

I AM GRATEFUL FOR...

img4

I AM GRATEFUL FOR...

img4

I AM GRATEFUL FOR...
img4

_____

What is it about your spiritual health that you are grateful for? Start with the
simplest aspect. Write a description and express your gratitude.

DATE / /

I AM GRATEFUL FOR...

img4

"For me, every hour is grace. And I feel gratitude in my heart each time
I can meet someone and look at his or her smile."
—Elie Wiesel

I AM GRATEFUL FOR...

img4

DATE   /   /

I AM GRATEFUL FOR...

I AM GRATEFUL FOR...

img4

I AM GRATEFUL FOR...

img4

I AM GRATEFUL FOR...

img4

> What is it about your emotional health that you are grateful for? Start with
> the simplest aspect. Write a description and express your gratitude.

I AM GRATEFUL FOR...

img4

"*The more gratitude I feel, the more I am aware that the supply is endless.*"
—*Louise Hay*

I AM GRATEFUL FOR...

I AM GRATEFUL FOR...

img4

DATE   /   /

I AM GRATEFUL FOR...

img4

I AM GRATEFUL FOR...

img4

At times of struggle, it can be hard to count our blessings. Recognize the
simplest positive thought, behavior, or action you experienced today.
Can you choose to be grateful? If you do, capture why.

I AM GRATEFUL FOR...

img4

"Gratitude is one of the sweet shortcuts to finding peace of mind and happiness inside.
No matter what is going on outside of us, there's always something we could be grateful for."
—Barry Neil Kaufman

I AM GRATEFUL FOR...

I AM GRATEFUL FOR...

img4

I AM GRATEFUL FOR...

I AM GRATEFUL FOR...

img4

I AM GRATEFUL FOR...

img4

Right now, wherever you are, what do your eyes notice? Write about this as if you were "seeing it" for the first time … with grateful eyes.

DATE   / /

"In the bad times, choose to grow stronger. In the good times, choose to enjoy fully.
In all times, choose to be grateful."
—Poetic Jay

I AM GRATEFUL FOR...

img4

I AM GRATEFUL FOR...
img4

I AM GRATEFUL FOR...

img4

I AM GRATEFUL FOR...

I AM GRATEFUL FOR...
img4

To be grateful is to acknowledge that someone helped us along
life's journey. Who helped you? What did they sacrifice?
Write about how you have benefited.

I AM GRATEFUL FOR...

img4

"*Interrupt anxiety with gratitude.*"
—*Danielle LaPorte*

I AM GRATEFUL FOR...

I AM GRATEFUL FOR...
img4

I AM GRATEFUL FOR...

img4

I AM GRATEFUL FOR...

img4

I AM GRATEFUL FOR...

img4

Who is the most unappreciated person you know?

How can you show gratitude to them?

I AM GRATEFUL FOR...

*"If you concentrate on finding whatever is good in every situation,
you will discover that your life will suddenly be filled with gratitude."*
—Rabbi Harold Kushner

I AM GRATEFUL FOR...
img4

I AM GRATEFUL FOR...

img4

I AM GRATEFUL FOR...

img4

DATE   /   /

I AM GRATEFUL FOR...

I AM GRATEFUL FOR...
img4

Self-gratitude: In what way have you helped to improve someone's life?
Describe what "gifts" you have and how you have
benefited. How have they benefited?

I AM GRATEFUL FOR...

img4

"*There is a calmness to a life lived in gratitude, a quiet joy.*"
—*Ralph H. Blum*

I AM GRATEFUL FOR...

img4

I AM GRATEFUL FOR...

img4

I AM GRATEFUL FOR...

DATE   /   /

I AM GRATEFUL FOR...

img4

I AM GRATEFUL FOR...

img4

Self-gratitude: What failure or adversity are you grateful for and why?

I AM GRATEFUL FOR...

img4

"Gratitude is an art of painting an adversity into a lovely picture."
—Kak Sri

I AM GRATEFUL FOR...

img4

I AM GRATEFUL FOR...
img4

I AM GRATEFUL FOR...

img4

DATE   /   /

I AM GRATEFUL FOR...

img4

I AM GRATEFUL FOR...

img4

Self-gratitude: List your top three values and describe
why you are grateful for them.

I AM GRATEFUL FOR...
img4

"Forget injuries, never forget kindnesses."
—Confucius

I AM GRATEFUL FOR...

img4

I AM GRATEFUL FOR...

img4

I AM GRATEFUL FOR...

I AM GRATEFUL FOR...

img4 I AM GRATEFUL FOR...

Self-gratitude: What are your top three strengths? Go to
www.authentichappiness.org or www.viacharacter.org and complete the free
(user name and password is required) VIA Survey of Character Strengths.
List your top three strengths and describe why you're grateful for them.

I AM GRATEFUL FOR...
img4

"Keep your eyes open to your mercies …
the man who forgets to be grateful has fallen asleep in life."
—Robert Louis Stevenson

I AM GRATEFUL FOR...

img4

I AM GRATEFUL FOR...

img4

I AM GRATEFUL FOR...

img4

I AM GRATEFUL FOR...

img4

I AM GRATEFUL FOR...

img4

Self-gratitude: Who inspired you? Describe how you have
benefited and the qualities you possess.

I AM GRATEFUL FOR...

img4

"Gratitude can transform common days into thanksgivings …
and change ordinary opportunities into blessings."
—William Arthur Ward

I AM GRATEFUL FOR...

I AM GRATEFUL FOR...

img4

DATE / /

I AM GRATEFUL FOR...

img4

I AM GRATEFUL FOR...

img4

I AM GRATEFUL FOR...

img4

_____

_____

_____

_____

_____

_____

_____

_____

_____

_____

_____

_____

_____

_____

_____

_____

_____

_____

_____

Self-gratitude: Who mentored you? Describe how you have benefited and the qualities you possess. Have you expressed gratitude to this mentor?

I AM GRATEFUL FOR...

img4

"Let us be grateful to people who make us happy; they are the charming gardeners who make our souls blossom."
—*Marcel Proust*

I AM GRATEFUL FOR...

img4

I AM GRATEFUL FOR...

img4

I AM GRATEFUL FOR...
img4

I AM GRATEFUL FOR...

img4

I AM GRATEFUL FOR...

img4

Self-gratitude: What contributions do you bring to your family? Describe
what they are and why you're grateful for them.

I AM GRATEFUL FOR...

"Wear gratitude like a cloak and it will feed every corner of your life."
—*Rumi*

I AM GRATEFUL FOR...

I AM GRATEFUL FOR...

I AM GRATEFUL FOR...

img4

I AM GRATEFUL FOR...

img4

I AM GRATEFUL FOR...

img4

Self-gratitude: What contributions do you bring to your community?
Describe what they are and why you're grateful for them.

DATE / /

I AM GRATEFUL FOR...
img4

_____

_____

_____

_____

_____

_____

_____

_____

_____

_____

_____

_____

_____

_____

_____

_____

_____

_____

"Gratitude changes the pangs of memory into a tranquil joy."
—Dietrich Bonhoeffer

I AM GRATEFUL FOR...

I AM GRATEFUL FOR...

img4

I AM GRATEFUL FOR...

img4

I AM GRATEFUL FOR...

img4

I AM GRATEFUL FOR...

img4

Self-gratitude: Do you have a relationship that has stood the test of time? Write about the qualities you have that help sustain this relationship.

I AM GRATEFUL FOR...

img4

RESOURCES

GRATITUDE MAPS ACTIVITY

The following Gratitude MAPS activity is an easy way to develop a framework for your practice and attain greater healing, health, and well-being benefits.

Mindfulness—With all the distractions in life, mindfulness is often difficult to achieve. In fact, distractions are some of the most common obstacles to creating a sustainable gratitude practice. Mindfulness, with origins in Buddhist meditation, is the ability to be aware of the present moment. In her recent book, *The Mindful Day* (2018), author Laurie J. Cameron describes mindfulness as deliberately directing our attention and mindset to our inner experiences, to others, and to our environment. Practice your own moments of mindful reflection on your blessings, abundance, and areas of positive energy. Using the space below, write down what you can commit to, and then schedule at least five minutes of mindfulness reflection.

Example: At some point during the week, take a few minutes to reflect on a positive event you experienced. In the space below, identify positive emotions you felt and why you're grateful.

_____

_____

_____

Awareness—With this greater awareness, your heart and mind are open to choose and acknowledge your mindful reflections and be moved to action. Create visual reminders at home or in your office to trigger you to take the next step and acknowledge your gratitude for the person or experience. Perhaps schedule a deliberate practice technique on your calendar. For example, schedule "Mindful Mondays" or "Thankful Thursdays." At such a time, commit to take action for your feelings of gratitude. Using the space below, write down one commitment you will make to help reinforce this awareness.

Example: Identify one person every Friday morning to call and express gratitude to or send a note of gratitude.

_____

_____

_____

_____

_____

_____

_____

Remember, the gratitude gap exists because people don't express their gratitude!

Preference—Being grateful for someone or something is rooted in your values. Your preference for how you express and practice gratitude must feel genuine and personal. Whatever your preference, it must fit you and your lifestyle. What are your *personal* preferences for practicing gratitude? You may prefer writing in this journal or drawing, painting, or sketching on the journal pages. Perhaps you want to include a gratitude meditation on a regular basis.

What are your preferences? _____

_____

_____

_____

If you're expressing gratitude to someone, consider how they would prefer to receive (hear) your message of gratitude. Is it a public or private expression of gratitude? Is it in writing or face-to-face?

Who is someone to whom you would like to express gratitude? _____

_____

_____

_____

_____

How and when will you express your gratitude to this person?_____

_____

_____

_____

_____

Specificity—The greatest benefits achieved by practicing gratitude come from your recognition and appreciation of specific people, experiences, and behaviors that are meaningful in your life. Once you've identified the preference, describe specifically why you're grateful for the person, experience, or behavior. Describe how you have benefited and specifically characterize the intentions, actions, and possible sacrifices made by the giver.

_____

_____

_____

_____

_____

_____

_____

Gratitude Letter Activity

Writing a letter of gratitude to someone who has made a difference in your life is one of the most highly recommended (and meaningful) activities for practicing gratitude. Identify an individual for whom you are grateful and describe *why*.

Be as specific as possible. Research shows greater health and well-being benefits are derived when you acknowledge the true actions of the individual, along with how you have benefited by their actions.

Name: _____

_____

_____

_____

_____

_____

_____

_____

_____

Schedule a gratitude visit with this person in the next week and plan to "*read*" your letter. (If you can't visit this person, call them. If they're no longer living, read your letter to someone who truly knew this person or someone close to you.)

How will I deliver this message (in person, phone)? _____

_____

When will I do it? _____

_____

_____

THREE EASY STEPS TO START OR SUSTAIN YOUR GRATITUDE PRACTICE

1) List the top three things you are most grateful for, at this moment. Use the acronym img4 (I am grateful for). *Be as specific as possible.*

img4_____

img4_____

img4_____

2) Identify one or two individuals for whom you are grateful and describe <u>why</u>.
Be as specific as possible.
Name_____img4_____

_____

Name_____img4_____

_____

3) Decide what you will do in the <u>next week</u> to show your gratitude for one or both of these individuals.
Maybe write a handwritten note or a gratitude letter and personally read it to them.
Be specific. What will you do and when will you do it?

1._____

_____

2._____

_____

Helpful Websites

DRW: https://www.drwcoaching.com/gratitude-resources/

Img4: www.img-4.com

HeartMath Institute: www.heartmath.org

Gratefulness: www.gratefulness.org, https://movingart.com/gratitude-revealed/

Emmons Lab: https://emmons.faculty.ucdavis.edu/

Greater Good Science Center: www.greatergood.berkeley.edu

Greater Good in Action: www.ggia.berkeley.edu

International Positive Psychology Association: www.ippanetwork.org

The John Templeton Foundation: www.templeton.org

Authentic Happiness: www.authentichappiness.sas.upenn.edu/home

The Positive Psychology Center: https://ppc.sas.upenn.edu/

Happify: www.happify.com

Apps

365 Gratitude

Gratitude Journal

Bliss

Grateful

MOJO

Thankful

ASSESSMENTS

The Gratitude Questionnaire (GQ-6):

http://www.psy.miami.edu/faculty/mmccullough/gratitude/GQ-6-scoring-interp.pdf

VIA Survey of Character Strengths: https://www.authentichappiness.sas.upenn.edu/home

For a variety of positive psychology assessments, go to: Authentic Happiness: www.authentichappiness.sas.upenn.edu/home

Gratitude Quiz: https://greatergood.berkeley.edu/quizzes/take_quiz/gratitude

Gratitude Resentment Appreciation Test:

http://www.midss.org/content/gratitude-resentment-and-appreciation-test-grat-revised-grat-and-short-form-grat

BOOKS

Robert A. Emmons
Thanks: How Practicing Gratitude Can Make You Happier
The Little Book of Gratitude: Create a Life of Happiness and Well-Being by Giving Thanks
Gratitude Works! A 21-Day Program for Creating Emotional Prosperity

Laurie J. Cameron
The Mindful Day—Practical Ways to Find Focus, Calm, and Joy From Morning to Evening

Rick Hanson
Buddha's Brain—The Practical Neuroscience of Happiness, Love & Wisdom

Jon Kabat-Zinn
Wherever You Go, There You Are: Mindfulness Meditation in Everyday Life

Sonja Lyubomirsky
The How of Happiness—A New Approach to Getting the Life You Want

Janice Kaplan
The Gratitude Diaries

Oliver Sacks
Gratitude

Diana Butler Bass
Grateful: The Transformative Power of Giving Thanks

Jeffrey J. Froh, PsyD
Making Grateful Kids: The Science of Building Character

David DeSteno
Emotional Success: The Power of Gratitude, Compassion, and Pride

Z. Colette Edwards, MD
Be Less Stressed

GRATITUDE VIDEOS/REFLECTIONS

Gratitude Heals Notable Quotes Video: http://www.img-4.com/wp-content/
uploads/2017/01/Gratitude-Heals-v2.mp4

Meditation on Gratitude and Joy—Guided Meditation, Jack Kornfield:
https://youtu.be/pZ_7oCGzwcM

A Meditation on Gratitude—Guided Meditation, Deepak Chopra: https://www.sonima.
com/meditation/meditation-on-gratitude/

A Gratitude Reflection—Guided Meditation, Linda Roszak Burton:
https://www.drwcoaching.com/gratitude-resources/

Gratitude Revealed: https://movingart.com/gratitude-revealed

About the Author

Linda Roszak Burton is an International Coach Federation, ACC Certified Coach and a Certified Brain-Based Coach from the NeuroLeadership Institute. As an outcome of her research and evidence-based coaching practice (www.drwcoaching.com), she develops gratitude programs and related img4 products to advance and advocate the health and well-being benefits of gratitude.

Linda is Founder and Managing Partner of DRW, Inc., a leadership development, executive coaching, and organization design firm. The firm's underlying philosophy is to help clients achieve organizational results by aligning strategic goals and organizational values through leadership development and employee engagement initiatives.

As a tribute to her late sister, Linda created DRW, Inc., her sister's initials.

"Healing does not mean the damage never existed.
It means the damage no longer controls you."
—Akshay Dubey

Breathe in love - Exhale gratitude